I WAS MADE FOR THIS WARFARE!

APOSTLE CARLA HARRELL

I Was Made For This Warfare!

HOV Publishing a division of HOV, LLC.
www.hovpub.com
hopeofvision@gmail.com

Front Cover Design by Hope of Vision Designs
Inside layout by Hope of Vision Designs
Editor/Proofread: HOV Publishing Editorial Team

Contact the Author, Apostle Carla Harrell at hornecarla76@gmail.com

For further information regarding special discounts on bulk purchases, please visit www.hovpub.com

ISBN Paperback: 978-1-955107-34-1
ISBN eBook: 978-1-955107-33-4

Printed in the United States of America

Dedication

I would like to express my gratitude to all the giants in my life, both big and small, for pushing me towards success and greatness. I would also like to thank my children and grandchildren, for being my inspiration.

Contents

Preface

I'm excited to share this book with you all. First and foremost, I give honor to Christ, who is at the head of my life. I'd like to begin by saying that in Volume 1, I touched on various highlights from my life. In Volume 2, I go into more detail for what the devil has been up to from the beginning of time to the present. This book aims to guide you on how to make it through and ultimately prevail.

Allow me to start by saying that being different

means you can't simply follow the crowd. Without understanding this concept, you'll continually fail. Wisdom doesn't come overnight; it's a daily journey towards understanding God's plan for you. As you live and learn, continue to discover your purpose. The more you commit to living for God, the more you'll realize He always has your best interests at heart.

The purpose for me writing this book is to assist those who may not understand that we are constantly under attack by demons aiming to destroy and demolish us. Demons are not friends; they are adversaries, and it's crucial to recognize the demons are all around you. The existence of devils and demons is undeniable. Do not doubt it or second-guess yourself—they are undeniably real.

Introduction

I often asked God, "Why me?" and He would respond, "Why not you?" He reminded me of His sacrifice, saying, "I loved you enough to die on the cross for your sins. When I walked the earth, I too faced trials and betrayals, even from those closest to me. I couldn't reveal their schemes until the right time so that I could serve as a living sacrifice for you. If I could endure the fire, so can you. Trust me and never give up easily."

In my younger years, I tried to fit in, thinking that

would bring me friends. It worked temporarily, but you can never truly please people—they will always find faults. They might even betray you because of who you are. Remember, it's not them; it's the devil knowing who you are and trying to deceive you into trusting him, making you stumble and doubt our Father. That’s why He commanded us to watch as well as pray; the devil prowls like a roaring lion, seeking whom he may devour.

Trying to fit in is like forcing a nail into a hole that's too small—you can try to enlarge the hole, but the nail will never fit properly. It's not about fitting in; it's about understanding that it's Jesus who enlarges your capacity, not the crowd’s approval. Jesus wasn’t popular, and following Him might lead people to dislike you, claiming you think you're better or calling you boring. Yet, those who seem to be friends can bring you down the hardest.

In this book, I discuss demons—a constant presence in our lives, battling against us. Did you know there are over 5,000 types of demons out there, causing torture and death? The flesh is weak, but armed with the Spirit, you can overcome these battles. Demons are drawn to our vulnerabilities—the things we see, hear, or engage with can invite their influence.

In volume 1, I shared that I was molested at the age of six and later experienced assaults by a demon known as an incubus. These encounters left me feeling dirty, scared, and powerless, often happening when I was most vulnerable—during sleep. Make sure you read volume 1, where I go into more detail about my assaults by a demon known as an incubus. This is a spiritual warfare where the enemy comes to steal, kill, and destroy, but remember, trouble doesn't last always. Even if you fall, you must get back up. God doesn't need cowards in His army; He needs warriors who stand firm even when faced with the unknown.

The devil thrives on your fear, attacking more fiercely when you are afraid. But there is One who is stronger than any devil or demon—Jesus. He can deliver you from any situation, rendering the devil powerless. Who do you serve? I serve a mighty God.

As you navigate this life, remember that seemingly harmless actions can lead to a lifetime of spiritual warfare. Choose wisely, resist the devil's temptations, and stay aligned with Jesus, who sees all and knows all. You might encounter people who, driven by jealousy or malice, might wish harm upon you, even using witchcraft to send demons your way. Recognize that our battle is not only against flesh and blood but against rulers and authorities of the unseen world.

This book is a call to arms, equipped with the knowledge and power of God, to stand firm against the forces of darkness that seek to disrupt and destroy our lives.

Chapter 1

See No Evil

Have you ever heard the saying, "What you see is what you get"? I used to see things I couldn't understand. Lying in bed, I'd watch my door slowly creak open. They would approach, and I'd cover my face. The demon's plan is to uncover you, meaning what you see can shake up your life. The devil is setting you up for failure because he knows you won't speak about what you see.

The Bible says, "For we wrestle not against flesh and blood, but against principalities in the air." The battle is both spiritual and natural. If the devil can keep you silent about what you see, you won't come out on top. People may start to think you're crazy, but that's not necessarily the case. Remember, the mind is the devil's idle workshop. Stay close to the strong, stay in church, be obedient, and distance yourself from those who are not for you.

The time has come for you to understand the intentions of the devil and his children. They want to keep you down, unable to speak out because of the weight of the world on your shoulders, unable to lift your hands because of your burdens. They aim to drag you further into the abyss. But remember, trouble doesn't last always.

Look at me—I'm a soldier for the Lord. You must go through the fire, but when you come out, your clothes won’t smell of smoke, and there will be no residue of being burned. God will be with you during your battle.

Chapter 2

Hear No Evil

Hearing is another way demons find their way to you. Phones are great for staying in touch with family and friends, but what you hear can change your life. You might call for one reason, and the conversation shifts unexpectedly. Through that call, a demon can transfer to you, making you feel ways you've never felt before. You might start doing things you've never done, thinking, "Something's not right. I've never acted like this."

By losing focus and listening to gossip, you allow the demon in. Before you know it, you're drawn to it. The demon then connects to you, bringing more demons, causing you to curse, cheat, or simply gossip. The demons have found an opening that grows bigger overnight. Understand, demons are not playing—they're coming for you.

Everywhere I went, something was always happening, and I didn't understand where it was coming from. Thank God for pastors who taught me how to stand strong. One person, in particular, my spiritual mother, Everlena Chisolm, made sure I knew, from a young age until now, that I can make it. She taught me to let God fight my battles, to trust Him and not doubt Him. Thank you, Mother, for teaching me to be a strong soldier for the Lord.

At work, trying to keep to myself, someone always approached me with trouble. My days would start off good until the enemy showed his ugly face. The enemy comes in all shapes and sizes, and the voices you hear may sound like loved ones or people you know. They are demons starting fires. Wow! I've said a mouthful.

Chapter 3

Speak No Evil

Be careful of what you say. Your words have the power to curse or bless; take heed, for you bring things to yourself through them. For instance, when someone asks, "Carla, how do you feel?" and you reply, "I'm not feeling well, I'm tired," you give the devil ammunition to use against you. I had to learn this the hard way. Stop saying negative things and start being positive. Even if you don't feel good, say, "I feel good," and you'll start to feel better. The enemy grabs hold of everything you put into the air.

Start speaking life into every dead situation, and you'll see things come back to life. When your life feels gloomy, adding Jesus into every aspect turns it beautiful.

The power of touch is significant too. You can transfer things through touch. When you buy items from rummage sales, you don't know what you're getting. From their hands to yours, something can transfer. One day, after acquiring such items, you might start to feel sick, sad, or depressed. Demons are spirits that can attach themselves to tangible things like clothes, money, cars, or even you. The things you touch become sources of energy that flow through you, continuing until you get delivered.

The enemy has fought me hard while writing this book because all his secrets are coming to light. Ever since I started writing, these secrets have emerged everywhere, in all shapes and sizes. Everyone who encounters this book will hear and see things because of it—I'm calling them out.

The gift of discernment is the ability to judge well and gain spiritual guidance and understanding. Discernment can be scary. I had to be trained to understand this gift. For example, in stores, I'd pick up on things I didn't understand. My head would hurt just passing people, or my chest would ache. I even went to the emergency room, thinking someone put roots on me. Each case is different; maybe you're coming into the full potential of your gift. Gifts come without repentance, meaning your purpose in life is another story altogether.

You can also sense spirits through smell. I used to ask God, "Why me?" He never answered, but now I understand. When you are chosen, you can't run or hide from who you are and how God made you.

Demons have been around since the beginning of time. One-third of them, along with the devil, were cast down from heaven because they wanted to take over. Remember, the devil can do almost as much as

God, but God holds all the power. Demons can mimic your children, your husband, and others. They can shape-shift to get your attention and cause you to sin. First, they need your trust; once they have it, they slowly move in to bring you down.

Shape-shifters can take physical form. That's what we're dealing with now—demons are stronger than before because we give them power. The devil knows his time is short, so he's targeting our children to destroy the youth, the future. Parents, watch your children and pay attention to them. We are responsible for our children. The devil and his demons know our fears and desires. They know what makes us mad, angry, or sad. He pulls these strings throughout our lives. The things we do as children come back to haunt us and our kids. Do you believe that? It's true. The words we say without thinking can curse our lives. We can speak blessings and curses upon ourselves. Demons are real. They look for dry places to live, seeking rest but finding none.

When you house a demon in your body, you lose control of your life. They control you, position you for failure, and lead you to destruction. Picture your insides being beaten and torn up; you're just a shell of yourself. Wake up before it's too late. The enemy comes to kill, steal, and destroy. Don't let him into your home or family. If you give him an inch, he'll take a mile.

As a child and now as an adult, I always saw black figures. I used to think they were my shadow, but they weren't. At night, I would hear and see things I couldn't understand. They tortured me, making it impossible to sleep. These demons, called night terrors, cause episodes of screaming, intense fear, and flailing while still asleep, often paired with sleepwalking. During night terrors, you try to wake up but can't. You walk through the day in a daze, unable to sleep, scared of what you've seen, and no one understands what you're going through. You look pale, like you're dying. I've been there.

Chapter 4

Challenges

On this road, there were many challenges meant to hinder me from going further. At times, I felt like giving up, and I didn't understand why I was going through all of it. My youngest daughter used to see spirits that terrified her so much she would run and get in bed with us. I remember one incident in Hazlehurst, at my ex-mother-in-law's house. We got in the truck and left. The devil wanted me and my kids dead.

As we drove on Uvalda Highway, the road was clear. Then, suddenly, I heard my oldest daughter scream, and I felt the wind rush past the truck. It felt as if someone had picked up the truck and moved it. The devil had other plans for us, but God stepped in just in time. What could have been a head-on collision, killing us all, was averted.

Chapter 5

The Bible

Thank God for the Bible, the roadmap that keeps me straight. The Bible was given to us to guide us in the right direction. Throughout its pages, you see how Jesus rebuked demons out of people and taught them how to stay delivered.

From the beginning of time, the devil and his angels have been roaming the earth, deceiving and controlling people's minds. It's scary, isn't it? For those who don't believe in demons and for those who do, know that they are lurking, waiting for the perfect moment to entangle your mind in the abyss. The abyss turns your mind to mush, making it impossible to control your thoughts or movements. Our brain is our CPU—without it, we are dead.

The devil only knows our past and uses it to keep us trapped in our old ways. He doesn't want you to know this, but you can break the curse. With Jesus, you can turn your life around. Don't keep repeating the same patterns as your family. God gives you the strength to change. Let's make good choices from now on and confuse the devil. Repeat after me: "My body belongs to God. Devil, you can't do more than I allow."

I remember when I was in a world of sin. I used to walk around blind, seeing only in the natural. The devil wants you to think that everything around you is okay and that the world is your oyster. But when you come to reality, you realize God has kept you through all the evil around you. I'm grateful today that He loved me enough to fight for me. When you take one step, He will take two. This means you have to want to change for God to come into your heart. You must try by repenting and accepting Jesus Christ as your personal Savior.

Chapter 6

Deception

Deception is a form of witchcraft; they interweave together. Demons come to deceive you, and they are even in the church. Some people lack the gift of discernment to recognize what's happening. These demons may look like your loved ones, but they are driven by a sinister purpose because they want you to trust them. They know that if they can resemble your loved ones or friends, they can get you to let down your guard.

Deception is the act of misleading someone. For example, they may claim to be a certain age but are actually another. Demons can get you to believe the lie because they are experts at lying. Earlier in my book, I mentioned that demons know your past—they do. They will bring your past to the forefront because they know what you like or hate. By exploiting this knowledge, they aim to entangle you further in their deceit.

Chapter 7

Life

I had to take a break from the book, and now I'm back. Let's talk about life. The enemy wants you to think you have all the time in the world, but you don't. God gave me a revelation: you're walking around enjoying life as if there's no end, thinking, "Oh, I have time." But I've seen people here today and gone tomorrow. In an instant, life can change. You must live your life as if it's your last day. Your life is like those dry bones until God comes in and breathes life into you.

Life may hit you hard, but you have to know that God is with you every step of the way. You can make it because He is carrying you every step.

As I lay in bed having sleepless nights, praying and talking to God, I often hear people talking and things moving around the house. It's usually around 3 A.M. I get up to walk around and pray. One night, I opened my room door and saw a pair of white eyes. I could see the shape and figure of a demon, but those eyes were unforgettable. When he realized I could see him, he vanished right before my eyes. They call that hour the witching hour. While you sleep, they lurk. Witches and warlocks are out making potions and finding you during your weakest hour. You're asleep and vulnerable. When something scares you awake, your heart races, and you're disoriented. That's when the demon is waiting. He already attached himself to you earlier in the week, maybe at your job. You've felt unwell for days. They come in pairs. One can do damage—imagine 5, 10, or 20.

I want to share something with you. God wants me to share it. After an argument with my sister, I couldn't stop crying. We have always been close. That night, God showed me a beautiful vision. It was a green garden with animals and trees of every kind. The hedges were short and groomed. Everyone got along—animals and humans together as one. God let me know that I had seen the Garden of Eden. It was so beautiful and peaceful. God knows just how to console and encourage you. The very next day, my sister and I started talking again.

Chapter 8

God Is In Control

So much is happening, and so much more is coming to this land. But God—what can we do but let Him be God? He will handle it all. Trust Him, let go, for He has the whole world in His hands. People and children are dying. There is so much evil, both moral and natural. Children are being raped and murdered. Just because of the color of your skin, people can kill you without a second thought, without a conscience. The worst is when a loved one is killed by a senseless act. You feel hurt, crying, screaming, and angry because you don't understand. "Why me?" you ask. "He or she didn’t deserve this."

Through all this pain and sorrow, think about Job. He lost everything he had. I hear you saying, "I'm not where you are spiritually." But listen, our kids were lent to us as a gift from God. The things that are happening, you can't do anything about them. God is love; the devil is of hate and doesn't love you at all. Remember, God is in control, even when everything seems out of control.

Chapter 9

When It's Hard To Let Go

Listen, I know it can be hard to let go of the things you think soothe you, even if they lead to sin. I've been there. Let God soothe, love, caress, and hold you. The enemy wants you to think it's hard to let go of sex, alcohol, lust, and other temptations. Look to your neighbor and say, "Change your mindset." If you make the first step, God will make two. People often say that God hears a sinner's prayer, but He doesn't hear it until we repent. We were all born in sin, and we need to get ourselves right for God to hear us. This means we need to repent and move forward in the direction God wants us to take. Repent, pick up your cross, and follow Christ.

Did you know sex was made for married people? I know you may disagree because it's such a pleasure. But when you have sex outside of marriage, you are fornicating and sinning against your own body. For one night of pleasure, you risk getting a sexually transmitted disease, HPV, cancer, or AIDS. Whatever is on your partner can come onto you, transferring demons between you and your lover. That's why, in the older days, many people remained virgins until marriage because it was sacred.

Nowadays, it's rare to find virgins. You are not alone; the enemy makes you feel that way. You might be scared to be alone, craving love. When you think you have that love, you might forget about Jesus, and He is a jealous God. You focus on pleasing your boyfriend or girlfriend, but it won't work. You can never truly please a man or woman, but you can please God.

Chapter 10

Your Past

That's just it—your past. From the beginning until now, the devil knew what was in your past. He brings your past into the present to work against you. The devil isn't playing with you; they come in packs. Don't be ashamed of your past, ever! Your past has been forgiven, saith the Lord.

For instance, as a child, I was molested.

Depending on the situation, it could have turned me away from sex, but it didn't—I ran to it. That opened the door for the demons, though they didn't start right away. Before I got married, I wanted to be loved, and I thought sex was all I needed. After I got married, I cheated, and it felt like a drug—I had to have it. It wasn't until I thought I had cancer that it stopped me dead in my tracks. I said, "Lord, I don't want to die in my mess and go to hell." What you did in your past can promote and elevate you for greatness because your testimony not only helps you but encourages others.

The enemy is waiting for you to let down your guard, ready to attack. Be careful what you accept in your life—acceptance allows demons to come into your life and spirit. Your body and spirit are sensitive;

whatever you entertain or attract will attach to you like glue, and no matter what you do, you just can't shake them off. Demons feed off fear, especially from your past. You may not want to go back to old habits, but you find them pleasing and want to return. That's called backsliding. What God has delivered you from, stay away from it.

It's been hard to come back and finish my book so you can be blessed and learn what the devils and demons are up to. The Lord has blessed me with two churches, and the enemy is mad. But who cares? Till the end of time, I will serve the Lord and be obedient. The devil and his demons have been fighting me; I have been in a spiritual and physical warfare. The demons are not just in the spirit; they are also in the physical, shape-shifting as your husband, children, parents, grandparents, etc. I hope you understand this because the devil wants you to be confused. They are out there walking with you and beside you, sifting and draining you.

My daughter had a preemie baby at six months; he lived to be four months old. Prayer kept him here so long, and he was a fighter who believed in God, even at such a young age. You see, distractions will come and go, but you have to keep your eyes on the prize—keep your mind on Jesus. The devil has no time at all; he and his demons are running out of time, trying to take you and your family out of the picture before their time. I don't have time to play with demons.

Let me tell you about my grandson, Truth Frey Merritt. The enemy knew who and what he would have been if he lived. Truth was diagnosed with Pulmonary Interstitial Emphysema (PIE), which means air is trapped in the tissues outside of tiny air sacs (alveoli) in the lungs. The doctors said his lungs looked like those of a 60-year-old smoker. Listen, the generation of this time is anointed and strong young men and women of God. If the enemy can wipe them out and kill them, they won't have a chance at all. Pray over your children and give them back to God. Yes, we had to go through the pain to have them, but they belong to God.

The Bible states, "Mother against daughter and son against father." This is already happening. Mothers are killing their children without caring, allowing their husbands to kill them. This is the world we live in. Yes, God created the world, but the devil is trying to take it over. Know God for yourself; learn of Him so you can't do wrong. Follow true leaders. Just because someone is family doesn't mean you can trust them. Families turn their backs on you every day until you learn who to trust. I thank God for my family when they were living, but now they are dead and gone. God knew what was best.

Demons are getting bolder and wiser every day. They walk with you, and by you, on the streets, appearing as friends, boyfriends, girlfriends, or children. Scary, isn't it? They are driven by a force from Satan. Did you know the devil teaches them his ways to bring you down and destroy you? Yes, he does.

They are called millennial demons—smarter and quicker than the average demon. Be very afraid and know their actions and tactics. The devil is mad at me for writing this book, but who cares? You need to know.

You might be going through tough times, but there is a way out, and His name is Jesus. The spirit of fornication is a tool through which an unclean spirit seeks to satisfy his own lust for power and fulfillment. That is why sex is for married people. Some people don't want to hear the truth, but the truth shall sct you free and make you whole. When you step out of bounds to satisfy your lusts, you make a huge mistake. That feeling of wanting to be touched, loved, and caressed will make you want that all the time because it makes you feel special.

Why do you think our children, when growing up and going to school, try to fit in? They will do anything to be part of the in-crowd. Yes, we've done it too. Have you noticed that no matter what we do, it wasn't enough? When you read the Bible, you see that God was not popular—His own kind turned on Him. If the enemy can cause you to be at each other's throats, not caring, not loving, talking about each other, he knows he has you right where he wants you. Did you know that every little thing you hang on to—lying, stealing, backbiting, cheating—comes with a price? Those are demons coming off everyone you encounter. You can be in the midst of such actions without doing anything, and those very things your friends say or do start to rub off on you. You start acting like them, talking like them, looking like them—that demon is very smart and cunning. Another name for them is familiar spirits. Familiar spirits are things we come accustomed to, and we lay down our guard.

Have you heard someone say, "I fell in love with the same kind of people who mistreat me"? That is called a familiar spirit. You can't help yourself until you have been delivered—those demons come for you, not the other way around. For example, my granddaughter was acting strange—she's a teenager. Remember what I said earlier—they go through a lot and try to fit into the world. We as parents and grandparents try to guide them right, but sometimes they have to learn on their own. We don't want them to go through what we went through, but sometimes we must pray and let them go and learn. I could see the demon in her and the way she was acting; it had her wanting to kill herself. I started praying, and later she came to me and said, "Grandma, I don't know what happened, why I was acting like that." I told her, "You were there, but it was a driving force that was controlling you. You had no control at all." That is what demons do—they control you.

It's about control; that's why our mind is the devil's idle workshop. He is always trying to hammer into your mind. Keep your mind on Jesus always. You've heard the saying, "Don't let him ride, or he'll want to drive." Demons are real. Be careful how you approach things and who you are around. Demons attach to many things.

Let me give you more examples. An 8-year-old child having suicidal intentions—meaning they don't know what causes them to act like that. Situations like ADHD, seizures, behavior problems, cancer, etc., are of the devil. Just thought I would bring that out. The 8-year-old told her parents and grandparents she wanted to kill herself. They asked why, and she couldn't answer. At times, she would just cry and scream. The family looked at her in dismay. I hope you see where I'm coming from. The demon in her is torturing the child's mind and heart because at times she doesn't feel like anyone loves her. Pay attention to your kids. Yes, she is young, but they are going through things too.

The differences between demons and spirits: demons are malevolent supernatural entities often described as fallen angels or minions of Satan. Spirits are considered ghosts or supernatural beings that cannot hurt you. What was Casper the Ghost? He was a friendly ghost. I love that movie, Casper the Friendly Ghost. He couldn't be evil or bad—he was sweet and nice. Demons, on the other hand, are demonic and evil; they come to make your life a living hell. Some people are already there and don't know how to escape. This is how: cry out to God, repent. "If my people who are called by my name will humble themselves and pray and seek my face and turn from their wicked ways, then I will hear from heaven, and I will forgive their sin and will heal their land" (2 Chronicles 7:14). We need to understand how to make it in these last evil days. Ask yourself these questions: Who is lying next to me in bed? Who is sitting next to me in my car? Who is working beside me on my job, talking to me every day? Is it Tanya or Thamuz, the Ambassador of Hell, demon, master of big weapons? You just don't know these days who you are entertaining. Watch as well as pray, because the devil can preach, pray, and speak in tongues. Know them by the fruit they bear. Know the spirit by the spirit.

Many people are drawn to miracles. Beware of people like Simon the Sorcerer in Acts 8:9, who boast of their own greatness. The miracle stems from the great I Am. He raised the dead, turned water to wine, healed, and set free. We must stay humble so God can use us.

Let me share with you a couple of demons you probably haven't heard about until now. One is the Soucouyant, a shape-shifting character who appears as a reclusive old woman by day. By night, she strips off her wrinkled skin and puts it in a mortar. In her true form as a fireball, she flies across the dark sky in search of her victim. Many demons can shape-shift into your friends or loved ones, torturing you with your past. They feed off your past because what you did back then empowers them now. They come back stronger and wiser.

You may get tired of hearing about Jesus coming back, but listen to me: with all this talk about demons, know that Jesus is alive and well. No devil or demon can match Jesus. The devil was cast down from heaven because he wanted to take over, but he couldn’t. God is our shepherd, and He knows what is best for us. Just know who you serve and who has you in the end.

Let's talk about the spirit of masturbation. Is it okay to do, or is it a sin? Think about this: masturbation requires desire. You must think about a certain person for it to happen. It is a sin. "But I tell you that anyone who looks at a woman lustfully has already committed adultery with her in his heart" (Matthew 5:28). "Everything is permissible for me—but not everything is beneficial. Everything is permissible for me—but I will not be mastered by anything. Food for the stomach and the stomach for food—but God will destroy them both. The body is not meant for sexual immorality" (1 Corinthians 6:12-13). Your body is for God.

I wanted to share something with you. I had to preach on Sunday, and then on Monday, the left side of my face was swollen. The devil is mad, but I'm not done yet. There is more to share about demons. Just because you are saved doesn't mean that the demons or devils will leave you alone. I was taught that if demons aren't bothering you, you are serving them. The things you hear and see are real. The enemy wants you to believe you are crazy, but you aren't. You may feel like you're not yourself at times. That is what they do—they cause you to wreck your life because they are in control.

I had a vision of walking through a house. A young lady told me, "See this door?" I said, "Yes, ma'am." She said, "This is the morgue. I want you to see it." I said I didn't want to see it, but she opened the door anyway. Inside, there were many children. I asked God, "Why?" He answered, "Disobedience, hard-headedness, stubbornness brought them here." "Train up a child in the way he should go (teaching him to seek God's wisdom and will for his abilities and talent), and even when he is old, he will not depart from it" (Proverbs 22:6). Stay in God, because without Him, you can't win.

Demons set up and form a line, waiting to terrorize you for years, taking turns until they get tired. Demons are like heaters—they keep you warm through your situation and then toward the end, they start getting cold, turning your life inside out.

Conclusion

In conclusion, understand that demons are not your allies. They have roamed the earth since the dawn of time, constantly observing and seeking opportunities to cause destruction. From the moment of your birth, they have been aware of your actions and your struggles. If you have not overcome these struggles, the demons will return, armed with more schemes and reinforcements to bring you down. It's a daunting reality, but it is crucial to remain vigilant and prayerful.

As the world grows increasingly tumultuous, you must guard against the temptation to harm yourself and stay strong in the face of adversity.

About The Author

Apostle Carla Harrell, aged 50, embraces each day as a precious blessing, grateful for the opportunity to fulfill her purpose. Her life is guided by a profound commitment to do the will of her Creator, whom she serves with a heart dedicated to His cause.

I WAS MADE FOR THIS WARFARE!

JOURNAL

I Was Made For This Warfare:

I Was Made For This Warfare:

I Was Made For This Warfare:

I Was Made For This Warfare:

I Was Made For This Warfare:

I Was Made For This Warfare:

I Was Made For This Warfare:

I Was Made For This Warfare: ________________________________

I Was Made For This Warfare:

I Was Made For This Warfare:

I Was Made For This Warfare:

I Was Made For This Warfare:

I Was Made For This Warfare:

I Was Made For This Warfare:

I Was Made For This Warfare:

I Was Made For This Warfare:

I Was Made For This Warfare:

I Was Made For This Warfare: ________________________________

I Was Made For This Warfare:

I Was Made For This Warfare:

I Was Made For This Warfare: ________________________________

I Was Made For This Warfare:

I Was Made For This Warfare:

I Was Made For This Warfare:

I Was Made For This Warfare:

I Was Made For This Warfare:

I Was Made For This Warfare:

I Was Made For This Warfare:

www.ingramcontent.com/pod-product-compliance
Lightning Source LLC
Chambersburg PA
CBHW071941210726
48293CB00004BA/1400

* 9 7 8 1 9 5 5 1 0 7 3 5 8 *